The Good Enough
GUIDE TO
BETTER LIVING

The Good Enough
GUIDE TO
BETTER LIVING

Leave Your Dishes in the Sink,
Serve Your Guests Leftovers, and Make the
Most Out of Doing the Least at Home

by Alison Throckmorton

CHRONICLE BOOKS
SAN FRANCISCO

Library of Congress Cataloging-in-Publication Data available.

ISBN 978-1-7972-1568-6

Manufactured in China.

Illustrations by Harrison Edwards.
Design by Henna Crowner.

10 9 8 7 6 5 4 3 2 1

Chronicle books and gifts are available at special quantity
discounts to corporations, professional associations, literacy
programs, and other organizations. For details and discount
information, please contact our premiums department at
corporatesales@chroniclebooks.com or at 1-800-759-0190.

Chronicle Books LLC
680 Second Street
San Francisco, California 94107
www.chroniclebooks.com

Contents

*My idea of housework is to sweep
the room with a glance.*

—Erma Bombeck

Introduction

Welcome to, if not the foremost guide on appearing to meet all the expectations in your home by doing the least amount possible, then a solid sixth-place candidate. Many tomes about home economics have been written—all focused on enhancing productivity and reaching household goals. Here, the author asks you to put away perfectionist ideas of potato ricers and pancake pens and direct your efforts to more noble pursuits, like napping, knitting hats for your guinea pig, or binge-watching true-crime shows while eating cheese puffs. Avoid the cleaning schedules and hospital-corner sheets and instead DIY (term used very loosely) your own sheets, napkins, and towels with the simple-to-follow instructions contained herein. Evade the pressures of entertaining and instead lean in to some light mendacity to achieve your home entertaining goals.

The domestic sphere is a kind of witchcraft, and true mastery of doing less can create the illusion of upkeep and the deception of cleanliness. Discover how to apply a filter to your home in the same way you might with a less-than-flattering selfie. By subtly and expertly redirecting the focus from the absolute chaos that is your everyday life, you can create, if not quite your dream home, at least one that does not cause you and your guests to wince when you step inside.

HOW TO USE THIS BOOK

Within these pages you will find not-always-tried and sometimes-true advice about managing the demands of your home. Settle in, comfortable in the knowledge that this guide expects very little of you. Read it cover to cover and apply every tip and trick to your life, scan the topics and interact with the ones that speak to you most, or read the book and do nothing with the information. *You* are the master of your domain.

The Kitchen

If you're alone in the kitchen and you drop the lamb, you can always just pick it up. Who's going to know?

—Julia Child

The kitchen is the hearth of the home and where it is estimated that the average person spends two thousand hours per year.* A well-appointed kitchen is a workshop and place of delicious creation. Why not lean in, using the least amount of energy and resources possible, and enjoy the ups and downs that are the savory delights of caramelized onions with the fecund sludge that is the salad bag in the very back of the fridge? There are no rules about knowing what you're doing—how you *appear* to be doing is all that matters.

*Author has guessed based on feeling.

KITCHEN UTENSILS:
A Replacement Guide

There are many kitchen gadgets and appliances on the market today, each with a specific use. As a result, the options can be overwhelming. Here are some replacements for the popular, yet fussy, implements one absolutely doesn't need.

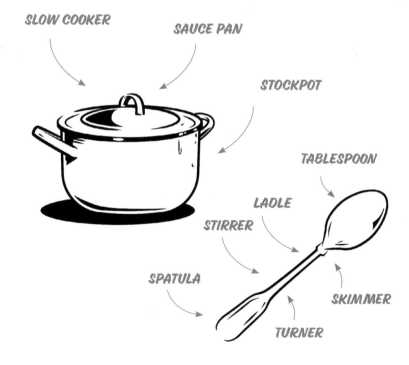

SLOW COOKER

SAUCE PAN

STOCKPOT

TABLESPOON

LADLE

STIRRER

SPATULA

SKIMMER

TURNER

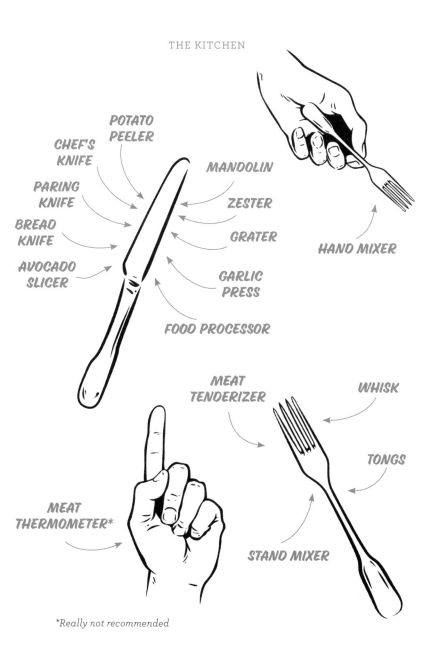

THE KITCHEN

POTATO PEELER

CHEF'S KNIFE

MANDOLIN

PARING KNIFE

ZESTER

BREAD KNIFE

GRATER

AVOCADO SLICER

HAND MIXER

GARLIC PRESS

FOOD PROCESSOR

MEAT TENDERIZER

WHISK

TONGS

MEAT THERMOMETER*

STAND MIXER

*Really not recommended

WHAT IS A CUP?
A Visual Journey

CUP (NOUN)

1. An open usually bowl-shaped drinking vessel.
2. Something resembling a cup.

Inside every kitchen is an important building block that should not be overlooked. We are speaking, of course, of the cup. Once it is established what a cup is (please see definition above), you begin to see cups everywhere (and not just the ones containing day-old water strewn about one's living space). More importantly, when we understand what a cup is, we understand it's the no-less-useful cousin of the bowl. And it is in this moment that the secrets of underachieving in the kitchen are truly revealed.
Take a moment to review the many different iterations of a cup.

CUP

DRINKING GLASS

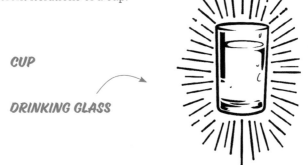

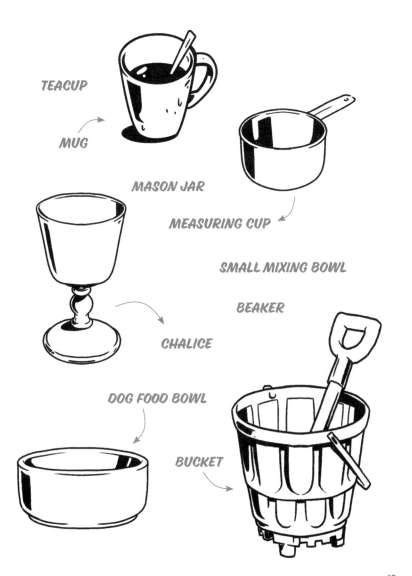

TEACUP

MUG

MASON JAR

MEASURING CUP

SMALL MIXING BOWL

BEAKER

CHALICE

DOG FOOD BOWL

BUCKET

Three-Minute Meals

TOAST WITH BUTTER

1. Take out two slices of bread.
2. Place in toaster.
3. Toast until desired color is achieved.
4. Spread each toasted slice with butter.
5. Enjoy your time-saving meal.

CHIPS AND SALSA

1. Take out and open a bag of chips.
2. Take out and open a container of salsa.
3. Dip or scoop chips in salsa.
4. Enjoy your quick, healthy meal.

LAST NIGHT'S LEFTOVERS

1. Take a fork from the utensil drawer.
2. Take container of leftovers out of refrigerator.
3. Leave refrigerator open.
4. Eat leftovers in the melancholy, pale light of the refrigerator.
5. Enjoy your mindless meal.

A FISTFUL OF CRACKERS AND A FISTFUL OF CHEESE

1. Take out a package of shredded cheese.
2. Remove one fistful.
3. Take out container of crackers (carefully, as you are now one handed).
4. Remove one fistful.
5. Stuff quickly in mouth, being careful not to choke.
6. Enjoy your budget-friendly meal.

15 OLIVES AND 8 STALE CRACKERS

1. Take out jar of olives.

2. Remove exactly 15 olives.

3. Put on a plate. (Optional: Put directly in mouth.)

4. Take out box of crackers from back of cupboard. (Note: Do not look at expiration date.)

5. Remove exactly 8 crackers.

6. Put on same plate as olives. (Optional: Put directly in mouth.)

7. Enjoy your waste-free meal.

HOW TO CLEAN THE DISHES

Always have clean dishes with these simple steps:

1. Fill the sink with hot water and soap.

2. Add your dirty dishes.

3. Forget.

4. When asked about them, respond, "They're soaking right now."

5. Forget again.

6. Repeat until you're dead.

INGREDIENTS:
A Matter of Perspective

Your pantry is a treasure trove of useful ingredients, even more so with a little imagination and a dictionary. Here are some ideas to get you started. (See p. 106 for menu ideas.)

REDUCTION

Also: Condiments

The savvy cook who doesn't want a sink full of dishes can find reductions through most common condiments. Ketchup, mustard, and Worcestershire sauce* all pack flavor without asking anything other than twisting off a cap. One can also dip their toe into deeper culinary waters and explore less common (though no less valid) "reductions," such as maple syrup and ranch dressing.

See "Puree" for additional sauces.

AIOLI

Also: Mayo with "other stuff"

Aioli is a numbers game: 1 + 1 = 2. Mayo plus another ingredient equals aioli. Add a few dashes of garlic powder to make garlic aioli or a squeeze of lemon and some capers to make a lemon-caper aioli. With the right attitude, one realizes that both ranch and Thousand Island dressings are, in fact, aiolis. If you're feeling bold, try your hand at ketchup, the "tomato aioli." The options are endless, and the stakes are low.

PUREE

Also: Sauces

We continue our culinary journey into the world of purees. Purees are just sauces. The most obvious choices rise to the top: sauces for pizza and pasta and sauces with the word *sauce* in them, such as BBQ sauce, cocktail sauce, and horseradish sauce. If we dig a little deeper, we can coax out a select variety of cheese sauces, such as jarred queso and Cheez Whiz.

FLATBREAD

Also: Any bread

Carbs make the world go around, and anything can be a flatbread if you deem it wide of surface and slight of thickness—pitas, tortillas, pizza crust, and English muffins all fall into this category. The end pieces of a sandwich loaf, too, could slide comfortably into this carby crew. Serve topped with peanut butter and jelly and you have a "flatbread with nut butter and fruit reduction."

GEMS

Also: Anything baked

The etymology of the word *gem* dates to the Gem company and their production of muffin tins in the early twentieth century. What that means for modern restaurants, however, is to call small, compact items of baked food "gems." For the home cook, such timeless staples as Tater Tots, chicken nuggets, and fish sticks all fall into this category. Serve to your dinner guests along with the etymology and they will be confused into submission.

PUFFS

Also: Anything fried

Puffs are a versatile addition to the home chef's tool kit. Often reserved for pastries and other fussy recipes, puffs are essentially food that has been fried. I direct you to the same timeless staples mentioned in the preceding paragraph—Tater Tots, chicken nuggets, fish sticks—except this time read the back of the package and realize they have been fried before being frozen. Voilà! Your "gems" now become "puffs," with minimal effort and maximum taste.

CRISPS

Also: Anything crispy and/or crunchy

Mouthfeel is an important part of the culinary experience, and one of the most recognizable mouthfeels is a crispy element. These foods are easily found in one's cupboard, if not in the dregs of one's skillet after forgetting to closely watch the bacon. Crackers, chips, cereal, and the small circles of cheese that have escaped the quesadilla as you flip it are all acceptable crisps.

MAC & CHEESE FORTY WAYS

With the right sort of attention, this culinary corner-stone can function with the same versatility as a little black dress. Fancy it up with premium cheese or go more informal with some processed meats.

1. Mac & cheese, plain

2. Mac & cheese with breadcrumbs

3. Mac & cheese with peas

4. Mac & cheese with carrots

5. Mac & cheese with broccoli

6. Mac & cheese with butternut squash

7. Mac & cheese with kale

8. Mac & cheese with tomatoes

9. Mac & cheese with potatoes

10. Mac & cheese with hot dogs

11. Mac & cheese with bacon

12. Mac & cheese with mortadella

40. Mac & cheese with garlic aioli

39. Mac & cheese with a bottle of crisp, white wine

13. Mac & cheese with bologna

14. Mac & cheese with chicken wings

38. Mac & cheese with small batch, craft beer

15. Mac & cheese with tuna

16. Mac & cheese with a cheeseburger and fries

37. Mac & cheese with a box of red wine

17. Mac & cheese with steak

18. Mac & cheese with pork chop

19. Mac & cheese with crab

20. Mac & cheese with shrimp

21. Mac & cheese with a juice cleanse

22. Mac & cheese with champagne on New Year's Eve

23. Mac & cheese with coffee on New Year's Day

24. Mac & cheese with ice cream

25. Mac & cheese with birthday cake

26. Mac & cheese with pie

27. Mac & cheese with caviar

28. Mac & cheese with potato skins

29. Mac & cheese with chicken nuggets

30. Mac & cheese with fish sticks

31. Mac & cheese with fish-shaped cheese crackers

32. Mac & cheese with a venti non-fat cappuccino, two pumps of vanilla, and chocolate foam

33. Mac & cheese with bottomless mimosas at brunch

34. Mac & cheese with a tomato reduction

35. Mac & cheese with potato gems

36. Mac & cheese with pizza

GROCERY SHOPPING:
Advice through the Ages

Food accounts for roughly 256% of the average person's household budget. Below, we explore ways to shop with economy in mind.

WITHOUT A LIST

To enter a grocery store without a list is to leave one's shopping to fate. These shoppers trek the aisles diligently, stubbornly believing that they know what they need—rice, chicken, and olive oil—yet exit the store with small-batch mustard, sponges, and four pounds of pasta.

WHEN STRESSED

Purposeful, decisive, and mildly irrational, the stressed shopper stalks the aisles, list clenched in fist. They rage internally and focus on the sweet and salty reward of snacks to soothe their big feelings. Much like those without a list and who are hungry, their future selves are left to deal with the fallout.

WHEN HUNGRY

The hungry shopper wanders the aisles looking for anything to satisfy the unreasonable cravings of someone who didn't snack before leaving the house. It matters not what's contained on the list in hand, for it was written by an entirely different version of themselves.

WHEN ON THE PHONE WITH FAMILY

Please refer to "When stressed."

AFTER A RAISE OR BONUS

The shopper newly flush with cash will adhere rigidly to their list. After all, they are dependable and responsible, and have been rewarded handsomely for it. Unfortunately, these shoppers will inevitably fall prey to the "artisan" versions of their usual staples: $20 cuts of grass-fed beef, $14 cheeses, and compact, visually appealing packages of uniquely flavored crackers that inevitably taste bad.

WITH CHILDREN

Please refer to "When stressed."

Do . . .
TRY YOUR BEST.

DIY Corner

HOW TO MAKE A KITCHEN TOWEL

Supplies needed:

- **CLOTH**
- **NEEDLE**
- **SCISSORS**
- **THREAD**

1. Cut a rectangle shape out of the cloth.
2. Thread a needle with thread.
3. Fold edges down.
4. Sew edges.
5. Use your kitchen towel with pride.

Skills to Master

The hallmark of one's success in the kitchen rarely relies on the ability to poach the perfect egg or prepare a mother sauce. Instead, if you've perfected even one of the skills on the following list, feel free to check it off and take comfort in the fact that you're well on your way to having true mastery over your kitchen.

☐ **Know the exact amount of pasta to cook—no more, no less.**

☐ **Fix weird-smelling ice cubes.**

- [ ] Anticipate the right time to stop the microwave before it burns/scalds/incinerates your food.

- [ ] Order DoorDash immediately after spending $100 at the grocery store.

- [ ] Have a favorite stove burner.

- [ ] Possess a can of "apocalypse" beans to be kept in the cabinet until the end of time.

- [ ] Own one partially burnt oven mitt.

- [ ] Keep a container of bay leaves, never to be used or discarded.

- [ ] Hold on to an old cookie tin that now contains anything but cookies.

- [ ] Have a clutch of tea bags that are essentially ornamental.

The Living Room

Live, Laugh, Love

—*A butchering of the poem "Success" by Bessie Anderson Stanley*

The living room is the largest space in the home, by landmass if not population. It is also the room that is supposed to suit everybody's needs all at once, for any possible activity, age group, time of day, or level of enthusiasm. This is a lot of pressure to put on a mere room. The key to mastering the living room is to embrace the concept of lighting, tricks, and overall, to acknowledge it as a space for basic domestic sorcery.

HOUSEPLANTS:
From Emotionally Unavailable to Unhinged

Plants are great additions to your living space. They can also be messy, dramatic, and time-consuming. Though at first glance one would think to choose plants that represent one's personal style, more important is to choose plants based on the level of shame and self-doubt you can manage at this point in your life.

SNAKE PLANT*

The snake plant is a housemate that never makes a mess, demands attention, or invokes feelings of inadequacy. Does your home have dark nooks or windowless bathrooms? Do you love the *idea* of plants but know deep down that you just cannot be bothered? The snake plant is the answer. Guaranteed to survive the Top Five Stressful Life Events, it tolerates being ignored surprisingly well.

WATERING (MONTHLY): Wait until you think it's time to water it. Forget. Remember and feel incredibly guilty. Go out of town. Return and water anxiously. Repeat.

LIGHT: Seriously, your snake plant doesn't care. Just leave it alone.

Author's choice for minimal interaction and commitment.

GOLDEN POTHOS

Golden pothos is the plant equivalent of the color beige: straightforward, accessible, and delightfully average. Keep your pothos in a small or large pot—it won't complain either way. It will climb or hang—whatever your aesthetic. Snip off a trimming, place it in water, and it will live happily almost indefinitely. This friendly plant wants to please.

WATERING (WEEKLY): The pothos's leaves will droop just enough to let you know it needs watering, but not enough to make you feel bad about it.

LIGHT: Any patch of light. No worries!

NERVE PLANT

Drama, excitement, frustration: Invite a nerve plant into your home and you'll have the plant version of a cat. Marvel at its ability to wither impetuously when you water it a few minutes late in the day. Carry it around your home weekly, looking for just the right place for it to thrive. You do not own this plant; this plant owns you.

WATERING (DAILY): Humidify, spray, water, measure, and monitor. The nerve plant demands the botanical equivalent of a Korean skin care routine.

LIGHT: Too much light and its leaves will burn. Not enough light and the vibes are off. Good luck.

WHAT IS ART? A SHORT LIST

Your living room is the outward expression of your personality and an opportunity to let your unique quirkiness shine. Adorn your walls with colorful teacup pig art. Cover every surface in succulents with aggressive spines. Instead of places to sit, simply offer squat, uncomfortable plastic crates. Anything can be art if it's weird, if you have a lot of it, and if you can't be bothered. What follows is a sampling of items that can be considered "art."

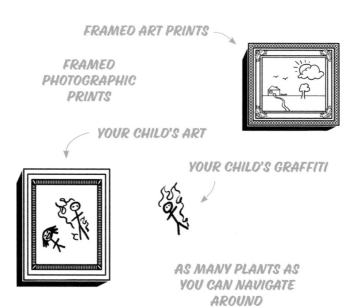

FRAMED ART PRINTS

FRAMED PHOTOGRAPHIC PRINTS

YOUR CHILD'S ART

YOUR CHILD'S GRAFFITI

AS MANY PLANTS AS YOU CAN NAVIGATE AROUND

FRAMED ART MADE
BY VARIOUS ANIMALS

FRAMED ART MADE
BY YOUR ANIMALS

SPOONS

THIMBLES

THIMBLES AND
SPOONS

AN UNCOMFORTABLE AMOUNT
OF ANTIQUE MIRRORS

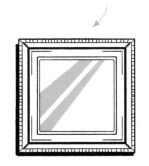

TAXIDERMY YOU RECEIVED
AS A JOKE AND HAVE BONDED
WITH EMOTIONALLY

CREEPY FIGURINES INHERITED
FROM YOUR GREAT-
GREAT-GRANDMOTHER AND
CAN'T GIVE AWAY NOR
AVERT YOUR GAZE FROM

CLOWNS

THE COFFEE TABLE:
Landscape of the Soul

While much of the living room space remains off-limits to the eager hands of strangers, a successful coffee table must be a tacit offering—to oneself, a partner, or a guest. Whether chaotic or highly curated, the expectation is for its objects to be picked up and mauled by whoever is sitting on the accompanying couch/chair/crate/floor. The following are some examples and ways to think through your curated space.

OVERSIZED PHOTOGRAPHY BOOKS, COASTERS, AND A CANDY DISH

This landscape speaks to an aspirational adulthood that doesn't quite exist. It exudes culture, hospitality, and a passive-aggressive request that one not get watermarks on the table. The candy dish is a whimsical touch, a nod to the halcyon days of childhood when candy dishes were bursting and waistlines weren't.

SCATTERED CEREAL, BROKEN CRAYONS, AND SIPPY CUPS

A home with these elements requires guests to tread carefully (and not just because plastic toy bricks are likely lurking on the floor). The inhabitants here are on the verge, either of a nap or a meltdown, and need support. Offerings of food and babysitting are welcome. Commentary on domestic matters and parenting are not.

ONE USED CONTACT LENS, A WAD OF CRUMPLED RECEIPTS, AND A SOCK

Despite initial appearances, this too is an expertly curated space. Though this landscape lacks both the refinement of the first and the harsh realities of the second, it possesses a je ne sais quoi that speaks to someone probably having a lot more fun than you. Do not underestimate this home. They are living (and likely laughing and loving, too).

Cleaning Tip

HOW TO CLEAN THE LIVING ROOM

Always have a clean living space with these simple steps:

1. Do not have pets.

2. Do not have children.

3. Do not have guests.

Display a piano to make people think
you can play the piano.

Frame everything, from your toddler's art
to your pet's art to your neighbor's art.

When in doubt, add another layer, be it a rug,
throw blanket, or decorative pillow.

Consider a neutral-toned pet to blend in
with any and all design choices.

Dim the lighting to make everything
look a little classier.

Remember that odors, pleasant or
otherwise, count as décor.

& Don'ts

Fill your home with artificial plants.

Fill your home with cats.

Fill your home to the point where
you can no longer fit in it.

Forget to clean your taxidermy.

Display anything you don't want to
have to explain.

Confuse hoarding with maximalism.

LIGHT AND MIRRORS:
Modern-Day Sorcery

The domestic equivalent of "smoke and mirrors," light and mirrors can alter the perception of reality. Utilizing both in one's home is an easy way to create the kind of effortless, moody atmosphere one sees on social media.

Light

A well-placed lamp can turn a stark living room into a cozy, creative space. It can do the same with furniture, too, making a couch that is past its prime appear as intentional as the most seasoned antique. Some light sources to consider:

NATURAL LIGHT

PROS: Free, available many hours of the day

CONS: At the mercy of local weather patterns, not available certain hours of the day, makes most evening-time activities impossible

LAMPS

PROS: Economical, easy to find

CONS: Boring, same lighting solution as your neighbors

LANTERNS

PROS: Unique, Colonial vibes

CONS: Major fire hazard, eventually becomes less unique and more annoying

Mirrors

When arranged correctly, mirrors will not only reflect natural light but will also trick guests into assuming that one's home has more windows than it does. There are a variety of mirrors available for home use. Here is a sampling to consider:

STRATEGIC

PROS: Inexpensive, utilizes existing natural light, clever

CONS: Complicated, needs many mirrors, involves algebra

OVERSIZED

PROS: Slimming, multiplies guests/inhabitants, a focal point for the vain

CONS: Expensive, heavy, potential to tip over and trap guests

FUNHOUSE

PROS: Fun, conversation starter, entertainment for children's parties

CONS: Terrifying, disorienting, could potentially conjure clowns

HOW TO MAKE A CURTAIN

Supplies needed:

- **CLOTH**
- **SCISSORS**
- **NEEDLE**
- **THREAD**

1. Cut a very large rectangle shape out of the cloth.

2. Thread a needle with thread.

3. Fold down the edges.

4. Sew.

5. Hang your curtain with pride.

Skills to Master

The success of one's living room is less about decorating prowess and more about the unsung heroes of the space. If you wish to remain on the path to domestic bliss, a living room must always contain:

- [ ] **A perpetually messy landing area beyond a mortal's ability to keep in check.**

....

- [ ] **A drawer full of cords and old tech, "just in case."**

....

- [ ] **A lamp that illuminates a 2-inch radius around the base and is, effectively, useless.**

- [ ] A large, unsightly stain covered by a decorative pillow, throw blanket, or strategically placed rug.

- [ ] A container of change, used for laundry, late-night snack runs, and emergency tooth fairy money.

- [ ] A lone, ineffective remote that looks exactly like the remotes that actually work.

- [ ] An exercise machine used as clothing storage, cat furniture, and/or a climber.

- [ ] Either one scented candle, or twelve. Nothing in between.

- [ ] Scattered tumbleweeds of dust (may contain pet hair, pillow feathers, potting soil, or food crumbs).

- [ ] Box of board games, each missing critical pieces for play.

The Dining Room

After a good dinner,
one can forgive
anybody, even one's
own relatives.

–Oscar Wilde

Please see: The Kitchen (p. 13); The Living Room (p. 37);
and, sometimes, The Bedroom (p. 63).

The Bedroom

If you're gonna fall apart, do it in your own bedroom.

—*Margot Kidder*

Much can be said about what happens in the bedroom, but we won't be saying any of *that* here. And besides, if a bedroom is living up to its full potential, then the majority of one's time in it will be spent unconscious. Depending on the overall size of one's living space, however, a bedroom may serve as more than just a sleep chamber. For some, it may also be an office. For others, particularly those in possession of multiple children, or multiple cats, a place to go and hide. To this end, it should receive the same respect as the bathroom— a place of contemplation and solitude—and time spent in the bedroom may be as reflective and meditative, or as raucous and chaotic, as meets one's needs at the time.

THE CHAIR

A ubiquitous part of a bedroom, The Chair stands sentry against the encroaching clutter all bedrooms face. Though never purchased and placed in the room for such purpose, The Chair (sometimes also The Bench, The Table, The Crate, or The Exercise Equipment) does double duty as a landing area for items not discarded by the front door; clothing of dubious origin; and materials gathered for eventual organization.

SEATING AREA

The Chair is used for many things, but never as a chair. To sit in The Chair is to experience a disconnect from reality, the feeling of viewing one's life from outside the body. From this unfamiliar vantage point, the flaws and questionable design choices of one's bedroom make themselves known. Why do I have so many throw pillows? (See p. 74.) Why is my nightstand so messy? (See p. 76.)

STATEMENT PIECE

A focal point of the bedroom, The Chair is often of superior quality and design compared to its more humble dining room brethren. Taking up residence in the corner, either with an understated grace or an ostentatious presence, its primary function is to direct the gaze from the unmade bed and cluttered dresser. Its secondary function, however, literally covers up its first: as a catchall for discarded items when one enters the bedroom. Jackets, purses, bras, books, and any items that belong elsewhere all call The Chair their temporary home. Never staying long, these items cycle in and out of this space on a weekly, if not daily, basis. Yet if one is quick enough, they may get a glimpse of The Chair's original grandeur.

OFFICE FURNITURE

When space is limited, the bedroom can function as a home office, with The Chair as its seat of productivity. But the comfort of working from one's bed is generally too powerful to resist, and The Chair once again becomes a repository, this time for office supplies. As you snuggle deeper in bed, smug in both your coziness and productivity, The Chair gathers files, papers, pens, and the nice blazer you wear over your pajamas in virtual meetings.

CLOTHING STORAGE

A final, inescapable function of The Chair is to serve as a laundry center. A folded pile of clean clothes, fresh from the dryer, finds its place on a clear surface of The Chair, to be picked from until only a few rumpled shirts remain. Gently used items (see p. 70) are hung or draped carefully on chairbacks or exercise equipment handles, "airing out" for use again the following day.

HOW TO MAKE A SHEET

Supplies needed:

- **CLOTH**
- **NEEDLE**
- **SCISSORS**
- **THREAD**

1. Cut a large rectangle shape out of the cloth.

2. Thread a needle with thread.

3. Fold down the edges.

4. Sew.

5. Fit your sheet on your bed with pride.

THE LIFE CYCLE OF LAUNDRY

It is easy for one to spend much of their free time managing laundry. Yet when we understand that cleanliness is a spectrum and not an absolute, we can break free from the tedious expectations of the "wash 'n' fold" drudgery and see the true wonder of this domestic life cycle.

CLEAN

After a day of moderate use and incurring no visible stains, clothing in this category can be classified as *clean*—a term that allows for a return to the closet or placement on The Chair (see p. 66) for another day's use. Undergarments, however, should be retired at this point.

USED

Items in this category carry the energy, and sometimes faint aromas, of the previous day's activities. If yesterday was a good day, re-wearing the same pants to re-create that good fortune is perfectly acceptable. One person's sweat stains on a black tank top are another's coffee stain on a white button-down. Do not justify your choices.

DIRTY

Eventually the sun sets on even the most rugged of khakis, and it is now time to say goodbye. Though "dirty" clothes should be placed in the laundry basket to be washed, this doesn't mean you must wash them immediately. Depending on the location of your laundry basket and current emotional state, items can rest here for as long as necessary. Go out and live your life. Your laundry will be ready when you are.

INCINERATE

A seldom-experienced category, usually known only to parents and pet owners, this is reserved for the most egregious of laundry disasters. Did your dog throw up on your favorite shirt from high school that you can finally fit into again, only to accidentally be slid under the couch to simmer in its toxicity for three weeks, prompting questions about the mystery smell, before being found by your toddler and dragged around the house? No amount of bleach or fabric softener will be your savior. Burn it and grieve.

HOW TO MAKE A BED

The Enneagram of Throw Pillows

1 THE PERFECTIONIST

Spartan and precise, Ones know that a simple throw gets the job done. Void of pattern and benign in color, this singular throw is a rigid and restrained nod to decorating norms. Ones make up 10% of the population. Coincidentally, boring throws make up 10% of the options at Target.

3 THE ACHIEVER

Charismatic and goal-oriented, Threes enjoy a reasonable number of throw pillows, tossed nonchalantly on the bed. Restrained in pattern and riotous in color, they display a tasteful yet enterprising understanding of decorating expectations. This is deeply rooted in a Three's need for the approval of others, which they attempt to gain through throw pillows.

7 THE ENTHUSIAST

Unhinged and hedonistic, Sevens fear missing out on an eclectic throw pillow. Soft velvets, frolicsome pom-poms, chaotic designs—a Seven wants them all. The only thing stopping them is the size of their bed. Though Sevens appear to be thrill-seekers, the true reason behind all the pillows is for them to hide in when they get home.

NIGHTSTAND ZONES:
A Delicate Ecosystem

Unlike its more polished cousin (see The Coffee Table, p. 46), the nightstand is a lawless land containing the detritus of our daily lives. To manage this chaos, we must impose a sense of order and organization, and to do this we must break the nightstand up into zones. Acquainting yourself with these universal areas allows for a better understanding of the interconnectedness of your nightstand's important ecosystem.

ZONE 1: One of the most recognized zones on a nightstand, Zone 1 is for reading material. Be it a towering stack of TBR (To Be Read) or a sheaf of electronic tablets, this zone should be both aspirational in scope (books covered in dust) and realistic in practice (tablets never fully charged).

ZONE 2: Hand salves and moisturizers, ibuprofen and allergy medications—Zone 2 is all about wellness. Eye masks, melatonin gummies, and lavender linen sprays gather to provide easy access to all the comforts needed for a full night's rest. During cold and flu season, cough drops and tissues share the space.

ZONE 3: Cutting a swath down the middle of the nightstand, consider the various dishes and cutlery that accumulate over the course of a few evenings. Half-drunk mugs of tea, bowls of chip dust, spoons tacky with ice cream—these all should be contained to Zone 3.

ZONE 4: Rings, hair ties, loose change, earbuds—welcome to Zone 4. We shed a surprising number of objects once we get into bed, and getting up to put these items in their place, however near or far, isn't an option. Level up and place a decorative bowl in this zone to collect these important items.

ZONE 5: Whether a classy carafe or a plastic souvenir cup, Zone 5 contains the water we will reach for at 3:00 a.m., gasping and parched. Note: It is imperative to keep Zone 5 separate from Zone 3, lest you mistakenly reach for the cold mug of day-old tea, shocking yourself fully awake, never to return to sleep.

Cleaning Tip

HOW TO CLEAN THE BEDROOM

Keep your bedroom neat and tidy with the following steps:

1. Grasp the door handle to the bedroom.

2. Close the door firmly.

BEDROOM

Skills to Master

This is not that kind of book.

The Bathroom

You learn a lot about people when you're sitting on their bathroom floor or on their toilet seat, rifling through their stuff.

—Emily Weiss

If one's home is one's castle, then the bathroom holds the throne. While we often neglect décor in this space, in favor of creating comfortable and attractive entertaining areas, the bathroom is where deep thinking happens and, indeed, the place where most great ideas are born. The bathroom is also the only room in the home where a guest is permitted to inspect every nook and cranny in absolute privacy. And because they will, it is worth thinking about how this most necessary and personal of spaces can best reflect one's tastes, values, and identity.

WHAT'S YOUR PLY?

 Disciplined, economical, and no nonsense, 1-plyers get the job done efficiently (most of the time). Instead of wasting money on a second ply, 1-plyers prefer to save their pennies. When guests are around, 1-plyers should remember it's a good rule of thumb to keep at least one roll of the good stuff on hand to put out when needed, as a matter of respect.

 Steady, reliable, and regular, 2-plyers are the backbone of the toilet paper industry. They have nothing to hide and nothing to boast. If there is work to be done, 2-ply is always willing to report for duty.

 Gregarious, extravagant, and cheeky, 3-plyers enjoy a life of luxury, even if confined to the bathroom. These multi-plying cavaliers may enjoy any manner of personal indulgence, including that delightful boost where one least expects it. These 3-plyers know the true value of experience and will not skimp when it comes to their bottom line.

Over or Under?

The way in which you set up your roll is very important in that it doesn't actually matter at all.

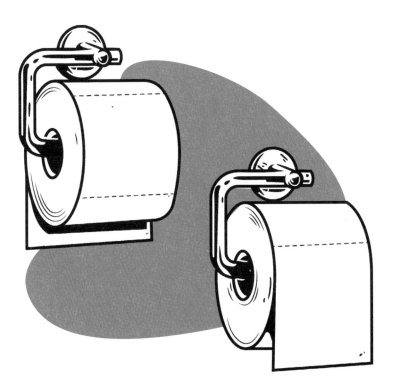

THE ART OF INTIMIDATION:
The Decorative Hand Towel

Adulthood intimidation is more readily available than one may think, and decorative bathroom hand towels are the hallmark of the apex predator. Trying to prove to your parents that you're a respected adult, despite needing help understanding health insurance deductibles? Hang some decorative hand towels. Laid off from your job and need a confidence boost that you'll get another one soon? Decorative hand towels. Having a party and want everyone to leave by 9:00 p.m.? Decorative. Hand. Towels.

Here are some timeless strategies for creating a bathroom to fear:

> **Choose towels that are slightly smaller than an adult hand. This creates a sense of disproportion when engaging with the towels—that one is too big or oafish to be allowed to use them.**

> **Choose towels that are light in color, preferably a white that is blinding enough to hurt the eyes. This creates anxiety that the towel will become dirty if one looks at it sideways.**

Consider styling your decorative hand towel with an intricate fold (see The Lost Art of Napkin Folding, p. 110).

Ideally the towels should have elaborately stitched designs—preferably matching the current holiday season—to create confusion about the best way to approach wiping one's hands: Use the embroidered front like a savage? Avail oneself with only the back, which isn't nearly enough surface area to get the job done? It is unclear and will remain that way.

Layer the decorative towel carefully, artfully, with other towels in the bathroom to create confusion about which towel, if any, should be used. The order is as follows: Bath sheet > bath towel > hair towel > real hand towel > decorative hand towel > washcloth > a final, smaller, even more decorative hand towel.

YOUR MEDICINE CABINET:
The Public Domain

It is a truth universally acknowledged that a person in someone else's bathroom will go poking around in the medicine cabinet. Rather than fear this intrusion, however, we must embrace the opportunity to be seen. It is a place of intimate lotions, potions, and pills, and the acknowledgment of our humanity. When one stares into the medicine cabinet, the medicine cabinet stares back.

Organizing your medicine cabinet is a biography writ small. Contained within are your struggles with anxiety and processing lactose, your sensitivities to both toothpaste and spicy foods, and the competing pressures of nail fungus and nail polish. Do not hide from these realities, for they are the realities that connect us all. There are, however, some simple organizational rules one should follow when placing items of such a sensitive nature:

BOTTOM SHELF

Though the eye is drawn first to the middle shelf, the bottom shelf should contain the most frequently used, and most benign, items. Nosy houseguests will begin their journey here, facing disappointment and the echoes of their own cabinet content. Here live toothpaste tubes with sticky white-and-blue residue, jewel-toned mouthwash, and mysterious face creams and serums.

MIDDLE SHELF

The middle shelf should contain elements that are of slightly higher stakes than the bottom shelf but familiar enough for prying eyes—drops for waxy ears, digital thermometers, nail clippers and nose hair trimmers, allergy medications, and antacids. Embarrassment on this shelf is meant to be low, except, perhaps, for how hard one walks the line of their expired medications.

TOP SHELF

The top shelf is where the gossip is at. As a matter of course, it's best to scatter more common medicines and accessories—an extra thermometer, a travel-sized bottle of ibuprofen, a mostly empty tube of Neosporin—as decoys to the true medical needs that reside here: tinctures for fungal, bacterial, and other embarrassing, though common, ailments.

Cleaning Tip

HOW TO CLEAN THE BATHROOM

Follow these simple steps to keep your bathroom clean:

1. Install a drain in the floor.

2. Hose down daily, like a kennel.

BATHING:
A Necessary Tradition

A timeless practice, bathing rituals endure as a matter of necessity in society. There are a variety of ways one can approach bathing, and the author provides a few in the following paragraphs without judgment.

THE RELAXING BATH

The Relaxing Bath is the closest thing to a spa experience one can get in their own home. Hot water, seasoned with essential oil–infused salts or a frothy foam of bathing suds, reduces aches and pains and alleviates stress. These baths are meant to be savored—with soft music, candles, and a good book—to experience peak relaxation before heading back into the fray beyond the bathroom door.

THE WORKING BATH

In contrast to the Relaxing Bath is the Working Bath. Aimed at productivity, the Working Bath serves more than one purpose. Not only is it the upkeep of the body—cleaning, clipping, filing, and exfoliating—it's also the maintenance of the tub and its environs. A Working Bath encourages a quick scrub of grimy grout, a wipe down of stubborn stains, and the rearrangement of soaps and shampoos to make one feel as if they've truly accomplished enough for one day.

THE SHOWER

The Shower exists somewhere between the Relaxing and Working Baths. Less than luxurious but more than economical, the Shower is a bathing sweet spot. Efficient and quick, there's not much to say about the Shower. Lather, rinse, and get out.

THE WIPE DOWN

Though not recommended as a modus operandi, the Wipe Down is an efficient way to achieve one's bathing goals in a pinch. Not unlike the approach to an especially muddy dog or a baby blowout, the Wipe Down is quick, perfunctory, and not a joy at all.

DIY Corner

HOW TO MAKE A HAND TOWEL

Supplies needed:

- **CLOTH**
- **NEEDLE**
- **SCISSORS**
- **THREAD**

1. Cut a rectangle shape out of the cloth.

2. Thread a needle with thread.

3. Fold down the edges.

4. Sew.

5. Use your hand towel with pride.

Pro tip: Decorate for maximum intimidation.

Skills to Master

As you move through your home mastering the necessary skills for each room, the bathroom—humble maybe, but no less important—should not be overlooked. Read through the following list, noting what you own, and marvel at your proficiency:

☐ **A small, dusty bowl of year-old potpourri.**

☐ **A fanatical attachment to a toilet paper doctrine, either Over or Under.**

☐ **A mangled tube of almost-empty toothpaste, inefficiently squeezed and guiltily kept.**

☐ A thermometer, its plastic cover lost forever.

☐ A dusty plant, either real or fake.

☐ A pair of seasonal, decorative towels,* gifted by a relative who comes around just enough to keep displayed.

☐ An uncomfortable amount of hair.

☐ A scattering of hair ties, visible only when you don't need them.

☐ A bar of fancy soap, gifted but not used.

☐ A small, aspirational library of reading material, unread and untouched since the invention of the iPhone.

*See p. 88 for usage.

Entertaining

What fresh hell is this?

—Dorothy Parker

Whether you're throwing a birthday party for your cats or practicing your culinary skills on feral offspring, it's time to take the skills you've learned thus far and put them to use in the fight cage that is Entertaining. Deft skill, sleight of hand, and low lights are necessary to set the stage for a successful dinner party. Menus that rival five-star restaurants, if not in quality then at least in name, combined with conversation of dubious veracity are key elements in rounding out a rewarding evening.

THE ART OF CONVERSATION:
Merriment and Mendacity

Entertaining is about more than menus and martinis. The key to an evening to remember is conversation that is both witty and engaging. Yet with the pulls of daily life—work, family, existential dread—one can't be expected to add "hosting" to their list of talents. Instead, consider embellishing the meager skills you already have. Were you reluctantly forced to do jazz band in middle school? Boring. Regale your guests instead with your experience touring worldwide with a now defunct, five-piece jazz band. There's no need to reveal *when* said experiences happened, only that they did happen. After all, time is meaningless. Following is some light mendacity to get you started:

Assertion	*Reality*
A gourmand who likes to navigate and consider various world cuisines	Ate six different kinds of frozen dinners last week
Manages and coordinates a highly opinionated team of creatives	Has children
A literary critic	Owns some books
Aspiring novelist	Owns many books
A poet	Has read a single poem
Life coach	Spent an undisclosed amount of time on the phone with a friend going through a break-up/job loss/major life event
One-time member of a singing quartet	Frequented karaoke bars with a few friends during college
Extensive experience in lifestyle finance and accounting	Helps mathematically challenged brother do his taxes every single year
Enjoys interior decorating while engaging in the principles of feng shui	Moved a geranium from one windowsill to another
Gymnast	Can still pick things up occasionally without groaning

MENUS FOR ANY DINNER GUEST

Hosting dinner guests doesn't have to be an anxious affair. The most important thing to remember is that it's not what you serve, but what you call it.

An Evening with Friends

STARTER:
Crisp bread with tomato puree dipping sauce and herbs
(Breadsticks with marinara)

MAIN COURSE:
Flatbread with tomato puree, fresh milk curds, and herbs
(Pizza)

DESSERT:
Gateau du chocolat with vanilla crema
(Brownies and whipped cream)

An Evening with Parents*

STARTER:
Little gem salad with lemon cream

MAIN COURSE:
Bavette steak au poivre

DESSERT:
Mille-feuille with crème anglaise

They paid for dinner.

An Evening with a Situationship/ Soon-to-be-Ex

STARTER:
Vodka martini with a twist
(Vodka)

MAIN COURSE:
Petite puffs of tomato puree, cured meat, and fresh milk curds
(Pizza rolls)

DESSERT:
Espresso martini
(Coffee with a slug of vodka)

An Evening with Children

STARTER:
Goldfish crackers
(Pesce-inspired, aged cheese crisps)

MAIN COURSE:
Cheese quesadilla
(Griddled flatbread with aged milk curds)

DESSERT:
Chocolate pudding
(Chocolate pot de crème)

THE LOST ART OF NAPKIN FOLDING

Napkin folds are an essential part of a well-designed table: the Bishop's Hat, the Fleur-de-Lis Goblet, and the Basic Napkin Stuffer are all common folds. Here, we explore a more exotic option, the Begrudging Boll Weevil.

STEP 1. Lay napkin flat.

STEP 2. Fold napkin in half the long way.

STEP 3. Fold sides in half again and over one another.

STEP 4. Turn napkin 117° to the left.

STEP 5. Tuck corners under.

STEP 6. Make sure tuck is tight.

STEP 7. Flip napkin over.

STEP 8. Take each of the four corners and fold out diagonally.

STEP 9. Tuck again.

STEP 10. Make sure tuck is tight.

STEP 11. Take a break but don't lose your place.

STEP 12. Flip up corners and have them meet in the middle.

STEP 13. Accordion-fold the napkin.

STEP 14. Fold the ends down to look like the summer home you'll never afford.

STEP 15. If you've lost your place, repeat steps 1 through 10.

STEP 16. Pick up napkin from the very center.

STEP 17. Turn napkin 73.5° to the right.

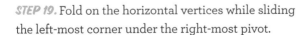

STEP 18. Take another break.

STEP 19. Fold on the horizontal vertices while sliding the left-most corner under the right-most pivot.

STEP 20. Place your expertly folded napkins on the table, but don't let anyone use them.

THE HOME BAR MADE EASY

Options for a well-appointed home bar can be overwhelming; however, all good cocktails can easily be broken down into the following three components: alcohol, mixer, and garnish.

ALCOHOL

There are hundreds of alcohol varieties to choose from, but when thinking in terms of ease, versatility, and sheer laziness, one clearly rises to the top: the handle of vodka in the back of your freezer. With a taste that's easy to disguise, and the fact that it's already in your home, you're on your way to a home bar worthy of a small dinner party.

MIXERS

Now that you have your vodka, it's time to think about what to add to it. Mixers function in many ways: hiding the taste of cheap alcohol, diluting a poorly poured drink, and giving color to an otherwise dull drink. Common mixers are sodas and juices, but there's no need to adhere to tradition! The door of your refrigerator contains an assortment of creative mixers to boost your cocktail credentials: maple syrup, BBQ sauce, pickle brine, and jam.

GARNISH

Though not entirely necessary, a simple garnish adds necessary visual distraction from an ugly glass and murky color. No need to keep fresh herbs on hand; with a little creativity, everyday household objects can serve as whimsical, decorative options: popsicle sticks with the drink's name written on them, a (clean) colorful barrette, a fake plant sprig, or garnishes saved from your most recent food delivery order.

HOW TO CLEAN
AFTER A PARTY

Keep your home clean after a party with the following steps:

1. Host the party at someone else's home.

SIDE DISHES: What They Are and How to Recognize Them

Side dishes are an important part of any place setting. The following are examples of acceptable side dishes to complement any meal.

SIDE DISH

SIDE DISH

SIDE DISH

SIDE DISH

SIDE DISH

SIDE DISH

SIDE DISH

SIDE DISH

MAIN DISH

CHARCUTERIE BOARDS:
The Lazy Host's Tableau

Charcuterie translates roughly from the French to "crap on a plate." A simple charcuterie plate needs only a serving surface (plate, baking sheet, or directly atop a clean dining room table) and various items from your fridge and pantry. Here is a sampling of charcuterie boards to fit your personality and lifestyle.

The "Leftovers" Board

1. Open your fridge/pantry and observe the contents.

- The leftover pad thai from when you binged Netflix for three days and didn't leave the house or shower.

- The container of olives you haven't opened since that one time you made vodka martinis and drunk-texted your ex.

- Dried-out marshmallows from the back of your cabinet, circa unknown.

- The remaining crust of gluten-free artisanal bread you learned to make during the pandemic.

2. Arrange on a plate.

3. Consume with the smug satisfaction of someone who is paid a living wage.

The "I Have Children" Board

1. Open your fridge/pantry and observe the contents.

   - The cheese you bought that your kids won't eat because it's "the wrong color."

   - The pears you bought accidentally, thinking they were apples as you rushed through the store while your three-year-old screamed. (No one in your house likes pears.)

   - The star-shaped crackers that you thought would not only taste the same as, but are more whimsical and healthier than, the name-brand fish-shaped crackers. You were wrong; they taste like garbage.

   - A handful of chocolate chips picked out of the cookies you made from a recipe your children have liked for years but as of Tuesday do not.

2. Arrange on a plate.

3. Consume with the smug satisfaction of someone who's used the bathroom alone within the last decade.

The "I Got a Bonus" Board

1. Pull from your shopping bag the ingredients from the super expensive boutique store you never shop at because it's super expensive and observe the contents.

   - The cheese whose name you can't pronounce and costs as much as your monthly cell phone payment.

   - The expensive fruit you never buy, and don't quite like, but you felt "fancy."

   - The crackers that no doubt taste the same as the crackers from the closer, cheaper store except the packaging is nicer.

   - The expensive, fair trade, artisan chocolate that won't fill the same void as the regular kind but will give you something to talk about at the office.

2. Arrange on a plate.

3. Consume with the smug satisfaction of someone who's throwing their future self under the bus.

DIY Corner

HOW TO MAKE A NAPKIN

Supplies needed:

- **CLOTH**
- **NEEDLE**
- **SCISSORS**
- **THREAD**

1. Cut a rectangle shape out of the cloth.

2. Thread a needle with thread.

3. Fold down the edges.

4. Sew.

5. Use your napkin with pride.

Pro Tip: Consider folding your napkin in a unique shape. (See The Lost Art of Napkin Folding, p. 110.)

ENTERTAINING

Skills to Master

Having conquered the skills needed to flourish in your home, it's time to show them off to your friends and family. Though entertaining can feel overwhelming and intense, a successful host has a range of tricks to pull from to make the experience a triumph. Explore the following deceptions to reach your full domestic potential:

☐ **Adjust the lighting and conversation to persuade guests to leave by 9:00 p.m.**

....

☐ **Serve the best food first (no one will remember the rest).**

- [ ] Always purchase the second cheapest bottle of alcohol.

- [ ] Exclaim "Oh, I think someone's at the door!" to remove yourself from awkward conversation or silence.

- [ ] Serve more drinks.

- [ ] Know that when children are involved, the gathering can only be "Fun!" but never actually fun.

- [ ] Keep literary magazines and bestsellers strewn about to appear well-read and informed.

- [ ] Wear black so food and drink can spill upon oneself without concern.

- [ ] Keep the lights low to enhance moody mystery.

- [ ] Own a pet that will only visit with guests who are allergic.

About the Author

Alison Throckmorton is a writer, editor, and domestic underachiever living in the Bay Area.